PRESIDENTS OF A WORLD POWER

A SOURCEBOOK ON THE U.S. PRESIDENCY

PRESIDENTS OF A WORLD POWER

A SOURCEBOOK ON THE U.S. PRESIDENCY

Edited by Carter Smith

AMERICAN ALBUMS FROM THE COLLECTIONS OF
THE LIBRARY OF CONGRESS

THE MILLBROOK PRESS, *Brookfield, Connecticut*

Cover: Franklin Delano Roosevelt's inaugural address. Black and white photograph, March 4, 1933.

Title Page: Inauguration of Woodrow Wilson at the Capitol. Black and white photograph, 1913.

Contents Page: Seal of the President of the United States.

Back Cover: United States Capitol, East Front. Watercolor by Paul N. Norton, 1971.

Library of Congress Cataloging-in-Publication Data

Presidents of a world power : a sourcebook on the U.S. presidency / edited by Carter Smith.
    p. cm. — (American albums from the collections of the Library of Congress)
    Includes bibliographical references and index.
    Summary: Uses a variety of contemporary materials to describe and illustrate the political and personal lives of the United States presidents from Theodore Roosevelt to Franklin Delano Roosevelt.
    ISBN 1-56294-361-8 (lib. bdg.)
    1. Presidents—United States—History—20th century—Juvenile literature. 2. Presidents—United States—History—20th century—Sources—Juvenile literature. 3. United States—Politics and government—1901–1953—Juvenile literature. 4. United States—Politics and government—1901–1953—Sources—Juvenile literature. [1. Presidents—Sources. 2. United States—Politics and government—1901–1953—Sources.] I. Smith, C. Carter. II. Series.
E176.1.P928 1993
973.91'092—dc20
[B]   93-15091
                                                                      CIP
                                                                       AC

 Created in association with Media Projects Incorporated

C. Carter Smith, *Executive Editor*
Lelia Wardwell, *Managing Editor*
Stacy Ferraro, *Principal Writer*
Elizabeth Prince, *Manuscript Editor*
Lydia Link, *Designer*
Athena Angelos, *Picture Researcher*
Shelley Latham, *Researcher*

The consultation of Bernard F. Reilly, Jr., Head Curator of the Prints and Photographs Division of the Library of Congress, is gratefully acknowledged. In addition, the assistance of the research staff at the FDR and Herbert Hoover presidential libraries is very much appreciated.

10 9 8 7 6 5 4 3 2 1

Contents

During his presidency, Theodore Roosevelt said,"I wish I could be president and Congress too." Several decades later, his cousin Franklin added, "He is not the only president that has had that idea." Friction between Congress and the executive branch has always existed within the American system, but it became especially heated during the first half of the twentieth century, as the nation faced many new and challenging problems. This watercolor shows the Capitol.

Introduction

PRESENTS OF A WORLD POWER is one of the volumes in a series published by The Millbrook Press titled AMERICAN ALBUMS FROM THE COLLECTIONS OF THE LIBRARY OF CONGRESS and one of six books in the series subtitled SOURCEBOOKS ON THE U.S. PRESIDENCY. This series chronicles the American presidency from George Washington through Bill Clinton.

The works reproduced in this volume reflect the extraordinary wealth of presidential documents held by the Library of Congress. The book also draws a number of images from the Herbert Hoover and Franklin Delano Roosevelt presidential libraries, which are administered by the National Archives.

Most of the documents which appear here are photographs, reflecting the major role that the camera played in shaping public perceptions of American presidents from Theodore Roosevelt on. The explosion in circulation achieved by the daily newspapers at the end of the nineteenth century under such publishers as William Randolph Hearst, Joseph Pulitzer, and others ushered in the age of "photojournalism." The demand for photographs of current events to illustrate these journals spawned a new kind of enterprise: the commercial picture agency. When such agencies as the Bain News Service, Herbert French's National Photo Company, and Underwood & Underwood sent their scores of photographers into the field, the White House was an important post on the tour of duty.

Advances in photographic chemistry and optics made for more portable cameras and faster exposures, resulting in a vast increase in the number and quality of pictures that a photographer could produce. The outcome of these developments was a highly detailed photographic record of the twentieth-century presidencies. Formal events of any consequence—and many informal—were documented on film. Posing with prominent visitors became a ritual of White House life, as did the president's annual appearance at the opening game of baseball season.

As the art of photography advanced, so the art of playing to the camera became an indispensable skill for public figures. For today's presidents, the "photo opportunity" is a basic tool of White House communications.

Historians now benefit from the wealth of photographs which document the presidency in our century. The works reproduced here are only a small but telling portion of the rich record of the American presidency, which is preserved by the Library of Congress in its role as the nation's library.

BERNARD F. REILLY, JR.

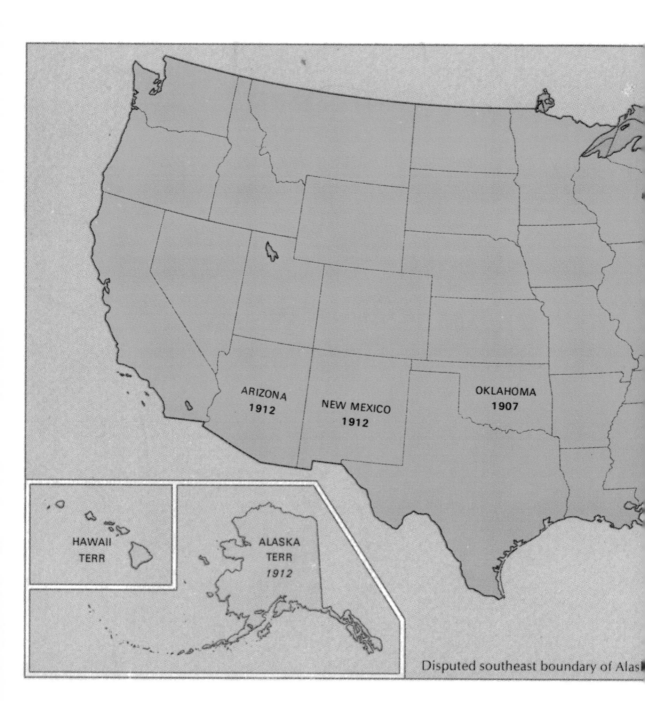

ARIZONA
1912

NEW MEXICO
1912

OKLAHOMA
1907

HAWAII
TERR

ALASKA
TERR
1912

Disputed southeast boundary of Alas

in 1903   1920

Between 1901 and 1945, territorial expansion slowed from the fast pace of the nineteenth century. Only three new states were created. The United States was now learning to manage its worldwide territorial holdings and to establish itself as a world power.

By 1912, the last three of the continental states had achieved statehood. Indian Territory was opened for settlement at high noon on April 22, 1889. A decade later, there were 800,000 settlers in the territory, which in 1907 officially became the state of Oklahoma. And in 1912, New Mexico and Arizona became the forty-seventh and forty-eighth states, respectively.

Through purchase and conquest, the U.S. had acquired a number of territories. Alaska, purchased in 1867, was organized into a territory in 1912 (its southeast boundary was settled in 1903). Hawaii had been annexed in 1898 and became a territory in 1900. (Both of these holdings would become states in 1959.) Also during this period the U.S. acquired Guam, Puerto Rico, part of the West Indies, and the Philippine Islands. These territories, many of which were thousands of miles from the continental United States, posed new challenges for the American government. Because the government was reluctant to admit that America possessed a colonial empire, no colonial office was established.

The Philippine Islands posed special problems because they were intended to be a temporary territory of the United States. William Howard Taft, who would one day become the president, was the first governor-general of the islands. Taft's honesty, intelligence, and loyalty to the Filipinos enabled him to benefit the islands under difficult circumstances.

THE PRESIDENCY

1901 President McKinley is shot and killed by anarchist lawyer Leon F. Czolgosz at the American Exposition at Buffalo, New York. Vice President Theodore Roosevelt becomes the nation's twenty-sixth president, at the age of 42.

• President Roosevelt invites African-American leader Booker T. Washington to be a guest at the White House—an action that angers many

Booker T. Washington

white Southern politicians.

1902 Coal mine owners agree to negotiate with striking miners only when President Roosevelt threatens to take over their mines. This is the first federal government action on the behalf of labor.

1903 At President Roosevelt's suggestion, Congress establishes a Department of Commerce and Labor, as well as a Bureau of Corporations. The Bureau will become instrumental in gathering evidence for anti-trust court cases.

• After an uprising led by Phillipe Bunau-Varilla and other officers of the Panama Canal Company, Panama secedes from Colombia. Roosevelt sends naval support to the uprising. Three days later, the U.S. recognizes the Republic of Panama.

1904 Promising a "square deal" for the people, Theodore Roosevelt easily defeats Democrat Alton Parker in the presi-

THE SCENE AT HOME AND ABROAD

1901 The stock market collapses in a panic resulting from a corner in Northern Pacific Railroad shares. Both speculators and average investors are wiped out.

1903 Orville and Wilbur Wright make the first successful airplane flight at Kitty Hawk, North Carolina.

1904 The Supreme Court rules that the Northern

Securities Company is violating the Sherman Anti-Trust Act and orders the company to dissolve. In 1911, the court orders the Standard Oil Company and the American Tobacco Company to dissolve on the same grounds.

1905 Socialist Eugene V. Debs founds the Industrial Workers of the World (the "Wobblies"), the first labor organization

formally committed to class warfare.

1906 Upton Sinclair's novel *The Jungle* is published. It describes negligence in the meat-packing industry and leads to passage of the Pure Food and Drug Act and the Meat Inspection Act.

• Over 700 people die in an earthquake in San Francisco. A subsequent fire results in about $210 million worth of property damage.

1907 Financial panic causes Wall Street prices to fall and leads to many bank failures. Financier J. P. Morgan leads a group of trust presidents in a $25 million pledge to salvage the banks.

• Oklahoma is admitted to the Union as the forty-sixth state.

1908 Henry Ford introduces the Model T, the first mass-produced auto in the world. Originally sold for $850, by 1926 the

Theodore Roosevelt campaign poster

dential election.
• In an address to Congress, President Roosevelt formulates the Roosevelt Corollary, an extension of the Monroe Doctrine which asserts the right of the United States to interfere in Latin American affairs in order to maintain peace and prevent European intervention.

1906 President Roosevelt is awarded the Nobel Peace Prize in 1906 for his role in mediating an end to the Russo-Japanese War.
• When revolutionaries overthrow the Cuban government, President Roosevelt authorizes U.S. military occupation of Cuba.

• President Roosevelt travels to Panama to observe construction of the Panama Canal. The trip marks the first time a president has left the United States while in office.

1908 William Howard Taft easily defeats Democrat William Jennings Bryan to become the nation's twenty-seventh president.

1909 President Taft is severely critcized for his support of the Payne-Aldrich tariff, which sets high tax rates for imported goods.

1912 In an unusual, four-candidate presidential contest, President Taft is challenged by the new "Bull Moose" Party candidate, former president Theodore Roosevelt, Democrat Woodrow Wilson, and Socialist Eugene V. Debs. Wilson is ultimately elected as the nation's twenty-eighth president.

price is an affordable $310.

1909 Explorer Robert Edwin Peary reaches the North Pole.

1910 Sociologist and African-American leader W.E.B. Du Bois founds the National Association for the Advancement of Colored People (N.A.A.C.P.), a group that advocates equality for African Americans.
• The census shows that the population

Henry Ford's Model T

has reached 92 million; less than half that number have high school diplomas.

1911 146 young women die in a fire at the Triangle Shirtwaist Company in New York City. The tragedy dramatizes the plight of workers and helps the International Ladies' Garment Workers Union to negotiate improved working and safety conditions in many factories.

1912 The British ocean liner *Titanic* strikes an iceberg off the coast of Newfoundland and sinks on its maiden voyage, killing 1,500 people, many of whom are American.
• New Mexico and Arizona are admitted to the Union as the forty-seventh and forty-eight states, respectively.

THE PRESIDENCY

1913 Congress passes President Wilson's pet bill, the Federal Reserve Act, which creates a new banking system based on regional divisions and authorizes a new type of currency, Federal Reserve notes.
• Shortly after taking office, President Wilson appears before Congress to make a case for his tariff reform proposals—the first time a president has appeared before Congress in person since Thomas Jefferson's administration.

1914 President Wilson declares America's neutrality in World War I and offers to negotiate peace between the warring nations abroad.

1915 President Wilson vetoes a Senate bill requiring literacy tests for all immigrants.
• When violence sweeps the Caribbean island nation of Haiti, President Wilson orders U.S. marines to land and restore order. The marines remain in Haiti until 1934, taking over most government functions. In 1916 the marines extend their occupation to neighboring Dominican Republic.

1916 Mexican revolutionary Francisco "Pancho" Villa leads a guerrilla band into New Mexico and Texas, killing sixteen Americans. Wilson sends U.S. troops into Mexico to punish him. The troops pursue Villa deep into Mexican Territory, but never succeed in capturing him.
• Wilson narrowly defeats Republican candidate Charles Evans Hughes in the presidential election.
• President Wilson breaks off diplomatic relations with Germany in response to that country's subma-

THE SCENE AT HOME AND ABROAD

1913 The 16th Amendment to the Constitution creates a national income tax; the 17th mandates the election of U.S. senators by popular vote (senators had previously been appointed by state legislators).
• On the day before Woodrow Wilson takes office, the Congressional Union for Women Suffrage marches on Washington, D.C., to demand the vote.

• The International Exhibition of Modern Art, or "Armory Show," opens in New York City. The show will have a profound effect on the future of American art.

1914 Austrian Archduke Francis Ferdinand and his wife are assassinated at Sarajevo by a Serbian nationalist. The murder leads to the outbreak of World War I.
• After eight years

Margaret Sanger at the birth control trial in New York City

of construction, the Panama Canal opens to shipping in August.

1915 The New York Society for the Suppression of Vice takes Margaret Sanger to court for writing and distributing *Family Limitation*, a groundbreaking work on the importance and methods of birth control. The court finds Sanger guilty and sends her to jail.

rine onslaught against American merchant shipping. Germany continues its policy of hostility and Wilson asks Congress to declare war in 1917.

1918 In a speech before Congress, Wilson describes his Fourteen Points program, a peace plan designed to bolster Allied morale and to assure the Central Powers of fair treatment after the war. The German government accepts the Fourteen Points as the basis of peace negotiations.
• After the Bolsheviks (communists) seize power, Wilson sends U.S. soldiers to Russia, where the troops of several allied nations are aiding White Russian (non-Bolshevik) forces in their effort to overthrow the new communist regime. The intervention is unsuccessful and all U.S. forces are withdrawn by 1920.

1919 In a unprecedented step, President Wilson personally attends the Paris Peace Conference. The Conference results in the Treaty of Versailles, which subjects Germany to backbreaking reparations and provides a charter for the League of Nations. Wilson receives the Nobel Peace Prize for his efforts in 1920.
• President Wilson takes his case for the League of Nations directly to the people on a national speaking tour.

President Wilson in a French newspaper

• President Wilson suffers a debilitating stroke. His advisers and wife carry out his executive duties for the remainder of his term.

• The American Telephone & Telegraph Company establishes the first coast-to-coast telephone hookup, linking service in New York with San Francisco.
• On May 7, a German submarine sinks the British ocean liner *Lusitania* off the coast of Ireland. About 1,200 dead are killed—114 of them are Americans.
• Charlie Chaplin stars in the comic silent film masterpiece, *The Tramp.*

1916 Denmark agrees to sell its Caribbean possessions (now called the U.S. Virgin Islands) to the United States for $25 million. Fear that Germany might buy the islands helps persuade Congress to ratify the treaty authorizing the purchase in 1917.

1917 The Supreme Court rules unconstitutional an ordinance in Louisville, Kentucky, imposing racial segregation.

• Congress passes the Espionage Act, which makes interfering with the war effort illegal.

1918 The Allies and Central Powers sign an armistice at Compiegne, France, ending the fighting in World War I.
• One out of four people nationwide comes down with the life-threatening Spanish flu. The epidemic kills nearly 500,000 Americans in the course of the year.

1919 The Eighteenth Amendment to the Constitution is ratified. Prohibition forbids the manufacture, sale, import, or export of liquor in the United States. The Volstead Act implements Prohibition and outlaws beer and wine in addition to liquor. (The Twenty-first Amendment repeals Prohibition in 1933.)

A TIMELINE OF MAJOR EVENTS
1920–1933

THE PRESIDENCY

1920 Advocating "a return to normalcy," Republican Warren Harding defeats Democrat James M. Cox to become the nation's twenty-ninth president. Socialist Eugene V. Debs receives one million votes even though he is in jail for opposing the war and the Espionage Act.

Harding campaign button

1921 President Harding names former president William Howard Taft Chief Justice of the United States Supreme Court, making Taft the only American to have served as head of both the executive and judicial branches of federal goverment.

1923 President Harding dies suddenly from a stroke. Vice President Calvin Coolidge becomes the nation's thirtieth president.
• In the first presidential message to broadcast to the American people, Coolidge announces support for a World Court and pledges to support Prohibition and lower taxes.

1924 Calvin Coolidge defeats Democrat John W. Davis and Progressive Robert LaFollette in the presidential election.

1928 Herbert Hoover, President Coolidge's chosen successor, defeats the Democratic candidate, Al Smith, by a landslide in the presidential election. He is the thirty-first president.

1931 In an attempt to end the worldwide depression, President Hoover gains a one-year moratorium on all

THE SCENE AT HOME AND ABROAD

1920 Reacting to the Bolshevik revolution in Russia, federal agents conduct "Red Scare" raids in thirty-three U.S. cities. The raids result in the arrest of more than 2,700 alleged communists, most of whom are non-political working-class immigrants.
• The Nineteenth Amendment to the Constitution is ratified, granting women the right to vote.
• The nation's first

A poster urging women to vote

commercial radio station, KDKA in Pittsburgh, Pennsylvania, begins broadcasting.

1921 The end of the wartime boom causes business depression and a high unemployment rate.
• The conviction of Italian-American anarchists Nicola Sacco and Bartholomeo Vanzetti for payroll robbery and murder results in worldwide protest by those who believe Sacco and Vanzetti are being prosecuted for their political beliefs. They are executed in 1927.
• Congress passes the Quota Act, lim-

iting immigration.
• Representatives from the U.S., Great Britain, Japan, and France meet in Washington and sign nine separate arms-reduction treaties.

1922 The era of the Harlem Renaissance of African-American writing begins with the publication of Claude McKay's *Harlem Shadows*.

1924 Congress passes the Snyder Act, which makes

World War I debts and reparations.

1932 President Hoover signs a bill creating the Reconstruction Finance Corporation. The RFC will dispense $500 million in loans to failing firms, especially banks and railroads, and lend $1.8 billion to the states for relief and public works.
• Seeking early payment of a promised cash bonus, about 17,000 World War I veterans, many of

The "Bonus Army"

them out of work and impoverished by the Depression, arrive in Washington. About 2,000 refuse to leave after the Senate fails to

approve a bonus payment bill, and President Hoover orders federal troops to break up this "bonus army."
• Promising a "new deal" for the American people, Democratic candidate Franklin D. Roosevelt defeats Hoover in the presidential election.
1933 Congress implements President Roosevelt's "New Deal" and creates a number of federally funded agencies aimed at ending the Depression.

• Roosevelt appoints Frances Perkins Secretary of Labor. She is the first woman cabinet member in U.S. history.
• The Twentieth Amendment to the Constitution is adopted. Among other provisions, the amendment changes the date for the beginning of the presidential term from March 4 to January 20.

---

all Native Americans born in the United States citizens.

1925 In the highly publicized "Monkey Trial," Tennessee school teacher John T. Scopes is tried for teaching Darwin's theory of evolution, which is forbidden by state law. Scopes is found guilty and fined $100.

1927 Aviator Charles A. Lindbergh makes the first solo flight across the Atlantic

Ocean aboard the *Spirit of St. Louis.*

1928 The United States joins 62 other nations in signing the Briand-Kellogg Pact which bans war as an instrument to enforce government poilcy.
• After years of struggle between Soviet revolutionaries, Joseph Stalin gains control of the U.S.S.R. and enacts a plan of rapid industrialization and state ownership of private farms.

1929 The stock market crash on "Black Tuesday" leads to the ten-year period of economic depression and mass unemployment known as the "Great Depression."

1930 Adolf Hitler's Nazi Party sweeps the German national elections. In 1934, Hitler combines the offices of chancellor and president, giving him supreme power over the nation. Hitler and fascist Italian dic-

tator Benito Mussolini are two of many political extremists who gain power during the worldwide economic depression.
• Novelist Sinclair Lewis becomes the first American writer to win the Nobel Prize for Literature.

1931 Treasury agent Eliot Ness gathers enough evidence to send Chicago gangster Alphonse "Scarface Al" Capone to prison for tax evasion.

A TIMELINE OF MAJOR EVENTS
1934–1945

THE PRESIDENCY

1934 President Roosevelt initiates his "Good Neighbor Policy" with the Latin American nations. It opposes armed intervention in American affairs by any foreign power.
• In a blow to President Roosevelt's New Deal recovery program, the Supreme Court declares the National Industrial Recovery Act—under which the federal government regulated wages and working hours in certain industries—to be unconstitutional.

1936 Franklin Roosevelt, running again with John Garner, defeats Republican candidate Alf Landon by a landslide.

1937 President Roosevelt is accused of attempting to "pack the court" when he proposes that the number of Supreme Court justices be increased from nine to fifteen.

1939 Physicist Albert Einstein writes the president to warn him that German scientists may soon develop an atomic bomb. The letter is the impetus for the creation of the top-secret Manhattan Project, which builds an American atom bomb.

1940 Roosevelt easily defeats Republican Wendell L. Willkie in the presi-

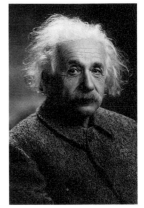

Albert Einstein

dential election. He is the first president to serve three terms.

1941 President Roosevelt per-

THE SCENE AT HOME AND ABROAD

1934 Angry public response to the 1932 kidnapping and murder of the son of Charles A. Lindbergh prompts Congress to make kidnapping punishable by death.
• Congress passes the Tydings-McDuffie Act, which authorizes independence for the Philippines, an American possession since 1898. (The Philippines finally become independent in 1946).

1935 Congress passes the Social Security Act, creating a payroll tax to provide for unemployment and old age retirement insurance for all Americans.

1936 Right wing uprisings against Spain's government begin in Morocco and spread to Spain. Francisco Franco leads the Falangists (Spanish fascists) against the Loyalists in the Spanish Civil War.

• Margaret Mitchell's *Gone With the Wind* is published.

1937 On a trans-Atlantic air trip, the *Hindenburg* explodes near Lakehurst, New Jersey, killing thirty-five of its ninety-seven passengers and crew.
• While patrolling the Yangtze River in China, the U.S. Navy gunboat *Panay* is bombed and sunk by Japanese warplanes; several Americans are killed. The incident is a sign of the growing strain on U.S.-Japanese relations.

1938 Congress creates the House Committee on Un-American Activities to investigate organizations and citizens whose political beliefs are seen as "un-American."

• Orson Welles broadcasts H. G. Wells's *War of the Worlds*, a fictional news report of an outer space alien invasion. Listeners

suades Congress to pass the Lend-Lease Act. The law permits the president to send massive amounts of aid to Britain, the Soviet Union, and other nations fighting Nazi Germany.
• The Japanese naval and air forces make a surprise attack on the U.S. Navy base at Pearl Harbor, Hawaii, on December 7. The United States declares war on Japan the following day. Three days later, the other

Axis powers, Germany and Italy, declare war on the United States.

1942 At the urging of the War Department, President Roosevelt orders 112,000 Japanese Americans into relocation camps. None are permitted to return to their homes until after the war has ended.

1943 President Roosevelt and British prime minister Winston Churchill meet at Casablanca,

Morocco, and agree to demand unconditional surrender from Germany and its allies.
• Roosevelt is elected to an unprecedented fourth term, easily defeating Republican candidate Thomas E. Dewey.

1944 President Roosevelt signs the Serviceman's Readjustment Act, or "G.I. Bill of Rights," establishing benefits for veterans after the war.

1945 Roosevelt, Soviet premier Joseph Stalin, and British prime minister Winston Churchill meet for the last time at Yalta to discuss the future of Germany and Eastern Europe and the establishment of the United Nations.
• President Roosevelt dies of a cerebral hemorrhage. Vice President Harry S. Truman becomes the nation's thirty-third president.

---

panic, mistaking the play for an actual news report.

1939 Germany invades Poland, beginning World War II between the Allies and the Axis powers.

1940 Hitler rapidly invades Denmark, Norway, the Netherlands, Belgium, and France.
• The latest census shows that the United States population has climbed to a new high of 132 million.

Adolf Hitler at a Nazi rally in Germany

1941 Hitler attacks the U.S.S.R., despite the existence of peace treaties between the two countries.

1942 Nazis begin the systematic murder of Jews in

concentration camps; over six million Jews will die in the Holocaust.

1943 Italian dictator Benito Mussolini is overthrown shortly after the

allied invasion of Sicily.

1944 The liberation of the rest of Europe begins in 1944 when the allied invasion of Normandy (D-Day) leads to allied control of France.

1945 Shortly after Hitler commits suicide, German emissaries sign an unconditional surrender at Rheims, France. The end of World War II is proclaimed the next day (V-E Day).

Copyright
1898 by
McLoughlin Bros

Part I
Prosperity and Reform

This illustration shows the twenty-sixth president, Theodore Roosevelt, as a lieutenant colonel and commander of the 1st U.S. Volunteer Cavalry regiment, popularly known as the Rough Riders. During the Spanish-American War (1898), Roosevelt and the Rough Riders won national attention by making a gallant charge up Kettle Hill, in Cuba, on July 1, 1898.

During the period from 1901 to 1929, Americans shifted their concern from the Western frontier to the nation's rapidly expanding urban centers. Many Americans were troubled by the growth of slums in the inner cities. They were also concerned about unfair labor practices in the workplace. The reformers who tried to change these conditions became known as Progressives.

After becoming president in 1901, Theodore Roosevelt used the popular reform ideas of the Progressives to expand the powers of the executive branch. Roosevelt was the first president to use his position to regulate big business and labor organizations. William Howard Taft, Roosevelt's successor, continued these policies.

Taft was followed by Woodrow Wilson, a former college professor who was regarded by many as being too idealistic. Wilson supported numerous measures that safeguarded the health and welfare of women, children, and the working class. In 1920, Wilson lobbied hard for the Nineteenth Amendment to the Constitution, which granted women the right to vote.

The traditional American policy of "isolationism"—which tried to limit U.S. intervention in foreign affairs, claiming they were not in the national interest—was interrupted by America's entrance into World War I in 1917.

The postwar years, during the presidencies of Warren Harding and Calvin Coolidge, were a time of economic growth and general prosperity. The boom of the twenties came to an abrupt halt, however, when the stock market crashed on October 29, 1929. The billions of dollars lost in the crash led to a series of bank and business failures that created a devastating national depression.

THEODORE ROOSEVELT

Theodore Roosevelt, Jr., was born in New York City on October 27, 1858. Roosevelt was named after his father, Theodore Roosevelt, Sr. (1831–78), a wealthy glass-exporter. His mother was Martha "Mittie" Bulloch Roosevelt (1834–84).

Young Teddy was a sickly child, afflicted with severe asthma. His illness was so bad that he often had to sleep sitting up to avoid choking. When he was only ten, his father counseled him: "Theodore, you have the mind but not the body . . . You must make your body." Taking his father's words to heart, young Teddy began working out in the gym his father had built in their home. He also learned to box, ride, hunt, and shoot.

Because he was too frail to attend school, Roosevelt was tutored at home by his aunt, Annie Bulloch, as well as other instructors. In 1876, he entered Harvard College. There, Roosevelt excelled both academically and socially. He was active in campus organizations and a runner-up for the campus light-weight boxing championship.

After graduation in 1880, Roosevelt married Alice Hathaway Lee (1861–84). Roosevelt enrolled in Columbia Law School, with the intention of pursuing a career in public service. He left law school the following year to run for the state assembly. He won a seat in the lower house of the New York State legislature in 1881 and was reelected in 1882 and 1883.

Alice Hathaway Lee (above) was the first wife of Theodore Roosevelt. When she died unexpectedly of Bright's Disease, a serious kidney ailment, at the age of twenty-two, Roosevelt drew a large cross in his diary and wrote under it, "The light has gone out of my life."

Theodore Roosevelt was born in this brownstone (right) at 28 East 20th Street, in New York City's historic Gramercy Park district. Another celebrated resident of the neighborhood was Herman Melville, famed author of Moby Dick.

WRITER AND RANCHER

On February 14, 1884, a double tragedy struck Roosevelt: His wife, Alice, and his mother, Mittie, both died at his mother's home. His wife died from Bright's Disease and childbirth complications; his mother was a victim of typhoid fever. Roosevelt retreated to the Dakota Badlands for two years, where he worked as a cowboy for the Maltese Cross and the Elkhorn cattle ranches.

Upon his return to New York City, Roosevelt made an unsuccessful bid for mayor. Roosevelt turned to writing after his defeat. He wrote two books: *Hunting Trip of a Ranchman* (1885), a vigorous account of his life on the Western frontier, and a biography of the politician Thomas Hart Benton (1887). In December 1886, Roosevelt married Edith Kermit Carow (1861–1948). Carow had been an adolescent sweetheart of Roosevelt's.

Roosevelt campaigned to elect Benjamin Harrison as president, and in 1889, the newly elected President Harrison rewarded him with an appointment to the Civil Service Commission. Reappointed by Grover Cleveland, Roosevelt served on the commission for six years. Roosevelt moved to Washington, D.C. when President McKinley appointed him assistant secretary of the navy in 1897. During one of the absences of Navy Secretary John D. Long (1838–1915), Roosevelt wrote, "I am having immense fun running the Navy."

Roosevelt wrote many books about his diverse interests, which included ranch life, big-game hunting, history, and politics. The volume pictured (above) is his fifth book, Ranch Life and the Hunting Trail, *published in 1888.*

After the death of his first wife, Roosevelt (opposite, top) traveled to the Dakota Badlands. "'Black care' rarely sits behind a rider whose pace is fast enough," he explained. Roosevelt was trying to say that he could outrun his grief if he kept moving at a fast enough clip.

After becoming president, Roosevelt asked a group of New York police detectives to pose for a photograph (right) at the president's country home, Sagamore Hill, in Oyster Bay. Roosevelt was proud of his work as New York City police commissioner, a post he held from 1895 to 1897.

THE "SPLENDID LITTLE WAR"

In 1897, when Theodore Roosevelt became assistant secretary of the navy, the Cuban revolution against Spain was under way. On February 15, 1898, the American battleship *Maine* was blown up in Havana harbor, resulting in 266 deaths. The American public demanded war, seizing the battle cry, "Remember the *Maine!*"

On April 25, 1898, Congress declared war on Spain. Roosevelt became commander of the 1st U.S. Volunteer Cavalry regiment, dubbed "Roosevelt's Rough Riders" by the press. Roosevelt and the Rough Riders distinguished themselves with a courageous charge on July 1, 1898, against the Spanish defenses on Cuba's Kettle Hill. Roosevelt's charge is often referred to as the capture of San Juan Hill, named for a group of hills nearby. Roosevelt became a national hero. Secretary of State John Hay called the conflict "a splendid little war" because it was so brief and so few Americans were killed in battle while securing additional territory for the United States.

Soon after the war, Roosevelt was elected governor of New York. Republican bosses who opposed him worked to promote the young reformer out of New York State with a nomination for vice president on the McKinley ticket in June 1900. McKinley and Roosevelt easily defeated their Democratic opponent, William Jennings Bryan.

The press gave a variety of nicknames to Roosevelt's 1st Cavalry division, who posed with Roosevelt (standing center, beneath the flag) for this photo. The nicknames included "Teddy's Terrors," "Teddy's Texas Tarantulas," and "Roosevelt's Rough 'Uns." But the one that stuck was "Roosevelt's Rough Riders."

This cartoon (right), titled "Roosevelt's Idea of Reorganization," shows the New York governor "stirring up a pot of politicians." By refusing to have his job dictated to him by the Republican Party bosses in New York State, Governor Roosevelt gained a reputation for being independent and headstrong.

As a child, Edith Kermit Carow (left) lived next door to Roosevelt in New York City. They had been playmates and, later, sweethearts. A year after Alice Lee Roosevelt's death, Theodore saw Edith at his sister's house, and they began dating. The couple became engaged on November 17, 1885, but kept the union secret for several months to avoid offending the family and admirers of Alice Lee.

McKinley and Roosevelt were rarely together during the campaign. McKinley remained in the White House while Roosevelt traveled the country, giving 673 speeches. This campaign poster (below) describes the McKinley/Roosevelt platform, which promised to place American money on the gold standard, meaning that all forms of U.S. currency would be backed by gold.

ROOSEVELT'S PRESIDENCY

On September 6, 1901, President McKinley was assassinated by anarchist lawyer Leon F. Czolgosz (1873–1901). Upon McKinley's death eight days later, Theodore Roosevelt took the oath of office. At 42, he was the youngest person ever to become president.

Roosevelt believed the power of the federal government should make life better for ordinary Americans. He put his beliefs into practice by attacking the trusts—business monopolies that controlled entire industries and crushed competition. Roosevelt earned the nickname "trust buster" for his successful legal actions against trusts in the steel, beef, railroad, and oil industries. When coal miners went on strike in 1902, he threatened to use the army to run the mines if mine owners didn't agree with the striking union. Most Americans approved of Roosevelt's policies, and in 1904 he was elected president in his own right.

Roosevelt favored a strong foreign policy for the United States, especially in Latin America. In 1904, he proclaimed what came to be known as the Roosevelt Corollary to the Monroe Doctrine. According to the corollary, the United States had the right to intervene in the affairs of Latin American nations whose governments were unstable. This policy was dubbed Big Stick Diplomacy, after Roosevelt's infamous comment, "Speak softly and carry a big stick; you will go far."

This photograph (right) shows the Roosevelt family (back row, from left to right): Theodore Roosevelt, Jr., Alice Roosevelt, and Kermit Roosevelt; (front row) Quentin Roosevelt, Theodore Roosevelt, Archibald Bulloch Roosevelt, Edith Carow Roosevelt, and Ethel Carow Roosevelt.

Roosevelt's sportmanship received national attention when, during a hunt in Mississippi, dogs lured a bear into a trap. Roosevelt refused to shoot the bear on the grounds that a trapped animal was not fair game. In a letter to his children, Roosevelt penned this sketch (below) of the encounter and noted that, while they had killed many deer, they were having "no luck with bears." The casual hunting trip eventually produced the "Teddy Bear." Named in Roosevelt's honor, the toy has comforted children for generations since.

The Bear Plays Dead

The Bear Sits Up

This cartoon (right) by W.F.A. Rogers appeared in Harper's Weekly on June 24, 1905. It depicts Theodore Roosevelt's negotiations between the Japanese emperor and the Russian czar Nicholas II after the Russo-Japanese War.

ROOSEVELT THE CHALLENGER

Roosevelt decided not to seek reelection in 1908. He chose as his successor William Howard Taft (1857–1930). Taft, who was nominated with overwhelming support by the Republican party, defeated Democratic candidate William Jennings Bryan (1860–1925). Roosevelt and his son Kermit embarked on a yearlong expedition in Africa, accompanied by naturalists from the Smithsonian Institution.

Roosevelt returned from Africa in 1910 and reentered the political arena. He made a speaking tour of the Western states, in which he criticized President Taft for being lazy and inefficient. Roosevelt made an unsuccessful bid for the 1912 Republican Party nomination. After losing to Taft, Roosevelt left the Republicans and ran on the Progressive or "Bull Moose" Ticket.

On October 14, 1912, while en route to a speaking engagement in Milwaukee, Roosevelt was shot by John N. Schrank, a German immigrant. The bullet passed through the metal spectacle case and the folded speech in Roosevelt's breast pocket and then through his chest. His fourth rib was fractured, but no vital organs were affected. "He pinked me," Roosevelt exclaimed. He then insisted on giving the speech before going to the hospital.

Roosevelt's candidacy fatally divided the Republican vote between himself and Taft, giving the election to Democratic candidate Woodrow Wilson.

This cartoon (above) stresses Theodore Roosevelt's power in the Bull Moose Party by depicting all the party's delegates as Roosevelt doubles.

During his yearlong safari in Africa (right), Theodore Roosevelt and his party killed five elephants, seven hippopotamuses, nine lions, and thirteen rhinoceroses. He also collected hundreds of diverse plant and animal specimens for the Smithsonian Institute.

ROOSEVELT'S LATER YEARS

After losing the 1912 presidential election, Roosevelt went on an extensive expedition through Brazil. In the Amazon jungle, he explored the "River of Doubt" (later renamed the *Rio Roosevelt*, in his honor) and collected plant and animal specimens for future study. During the trip he contracted malaria and suffered a severe gash in the leg. His leg became infected and never fully healed.

After returning to Sagamore Hill, Roosevelt resumed his writing and published several books and magazine articles. From 1910 to 1914 he was associate editor of *Outlook* magazine, and from 1917 on he was a regular contributor to the Kansas City *Star*.

Roosevelt's last involvement in American politics occurred when World War I broke out in Europe. He called for America to join the fight. After the United States entered the war in 1917, Roosevelt offered to raise his own volunteer force. President Wilson felt Roosevelt was too old to be of use in the conflict and refused to approve the idea. Roosevelt angrily responded, "I am the only one he has kept out of war."

During his later years, Roosevelt was plagued by illness, including recurrences of malaria and the leg infection contracted in Brazil. He died in his sleep on January 6, 1919. His son Archie cabled his brothers, who were members of the armed forces in France, "The Lion is dead."

This photograph (above) shows Theodore Roosevelt in his study, where he spent much of his free time reading and writing. Roosevelt once said, "I find it a great comfort to like all kinds of books and be able to get half an hour or an hour's complete rest and complete detachment from the fighting of the moment."

Roosevelt felt a strong commitment to conservation of natural resources. As president, he reserved 125 million acres of national forests, 68 million acres of coal lands, and 2,500 water power sites as protected national resources. Pictured here (opposite, top) is a lithograph of Yosemite National Park, in California, which became a national park in 1906 under Roosevelt's administration.

Roosevelt and his family spent many vacations at Sagamore Hill, their country estate (right) in Oyster Bay, Long Island, New York. While on holiday, he played polo with great enthusiasm. Roosevelt was so spirited a player that he was frequently knocked senseless from his falls.

WILLIAM HOWARD TAFT

William Howard Taft was born on September 15, 1857, in Cincinnati, Ohio. His parents were Alphonso Taft (1810–91) and Louisa "Louise" Maria Torrey Taft (1827–1907). Taft was an enthusiastic baseball player. He was an especially good hitter but, because of his size, he made an awkward runner, which hurt his game. A lifelong baseball fan, Taft introduced the American tradition of the president tossing out the first ball at the opening game of the professional baseball season.

Taft was an excellent student; he graduated second in his high school class with a four-year grade average of 91.5. He was also salutatorian (ranked second) in the class of 1878 at Yale. He later attended the University of Cincinnati Law School and was admitted to the bar in May 1880, even before completing his law degree. On June 19, 1886, Taft married Helen "Nellie" Herron (1861–1943) at the bride's home.

Once he discovered that he had a talent for the judiciary, a seat on the Supreme Court became Taft's career goal. He was later appointed judge of the Ohio Superior Court (1887–90), U.S. solicitor general (1890), and federal circuit judge (1892–1900). In 1901, President McKinley appointed Taft governor general of the newly acquired Philippine islands.

William Howard Taft was born in this spacious home (opposite, top) in Cincinnati, Ohio, on September 15, 1857. Taft was a large child who earned the nickname "Big Lub" from his brothers and sisters. As an adult, he often weighed as much as 330 pounds.

Taft's early interest in politics is suggested by this tribute (right) to the Democratic Party, written while he was an undergraduate at Yale. Taft's entry into politics represented a departure from family tradition: Both his father and grandfather had been judges.

The Vitality of the Democratic Party. Its Causes.

Before the result of the late insatisfactory campaign became known, the editorial columns of the independent press were constantly prophesying the general breaking up of parties, whatever the result. If Tilden were defeated, the eastern and western Democrats, who even up to this time had been held together only by the master hand of their standard bearer, would split on the financial issues. If Tilden were elected, he would disregard party ties and recognize in his appointments and plans the liberal element in both parties. General good feeling was to prevail, save among the extremists on both sides, and two different parties were to rise up from the mingled ashes of the old to fight political battles on new issues.

WILLIAM HOWARD TAFT: THE PRESIDENCY

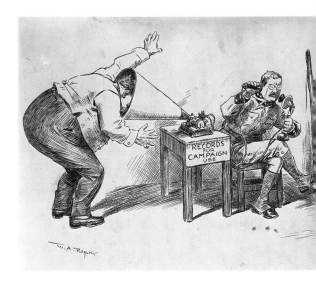

As governor general of the Philippines, Taft distinguished himself by speaking out for the Filipino people. He put down an insurrection, reformed a corrupt court system, opened English-language schools, and upgraded health care standards. Taft felt so loyal to the Philippines that he turned down two offers for a seat on the Supreme Court, once his major ambition.

In 1904, President Roosevelt appointed Taft secretary of war. During the next four years, Taft became a close friend of Roosevelt's and a staunch supporter of the Roosevelt administration. Once he performed double duty by serving as acting secretary of state in 1905 during the illness of Secretary John Hay (1838–1905).

With the urging of Theodore Roosevelt, his wife Nellie, and the Republican party, Taft accepted the Republican nomination in 1908.

Taft's administration was generally committed to Roosevelt's policies. However, some of Roosevelt's supporters felt that Taft was too conservative. They criticized his support for the Payne-Aldrich Tariff Act (import tax), which they felt favored business interests. This group of dissenters eventually split off from the Republicans and created the Progressive Party.

Taft was haunted by the larger than life legacy of Theodore Roosevelt. In this cartoon (above) Roosevelt is seen shouting, "Louder!" to a frantic Taft, who is trying to make his own "Records for Campaign Use." The Big Stick diplomacy advocated by Roosevelt has been laid to rest by Taft, symbolized by the club abandoned in the cartoon's right corner.

This 1909 photograph (opposite, top) shows William Howard and Helen Herron Taft riding to his inauguration. Taft was the first president to have a presidential automobile.

"Pauline," the presidential cow, is shown (right), grazing in front of the State Department. Pauline furnished fresh milk and cream for the Taft household. The Tafts were the last to have a presidential cow.

WILLIAM HOWARD TAFT: LATER YEARS

After being defeated by Democratic candidate Woodrow Wilson in 1912, Taft accepted a position as a law professor at Yale University (1913–21), where he taught government and international law. In 1918, President Wilson appointed Taft co-chairman of the National War Labor Board.

Taft still yearned to serve on the Supreme Court and, in 1921, his wish was fulfilled. President Warren G. Harding (1865–1923) appointed him chief justice of the United States Supreme Court. Taft was the first man in American history to serve as both president and chief justice. Taft enjoyed his new position, writing, "The truth is that in my present life, I don't remember that I was ever president." Taft was also an efficient judge: He wrote 253 opinions during his nine-year term.

Due to failing health, Taft retired from the court in 1930. His health deteriorated quickly, and on March 8, 1930, he died in his sleep. Taft's was the first presidential funeral to be broadcast on the radio. He was buried at Arlington National Cemetery, first of the only two presidents—the second was John F. Kennedy—buried there.

During one dinner at the White House with the Tafts, President Roosevelt cast himself as a clairvoyant and began to chant, "I see a man weighing 350 pounds. There is something hanging over his head . . . I cannot make out what it is." "Make it the chief justiceship!" cried Taft. Taft (right), shown with his wife, finally realized his ambition when Warren Harding named him chief justice of the Supreme Court.

On November 8, 1930, a delegation of Boy Scouts assembled at the grave of William Howard Taft in Arlington National Cemetery (below) to pay their respects.

WOODROW WILSON

Thomas Woodrow Wilson was born in Staunton, Virginia, on December 28, 1856. He was named after his grandfather, the Reverend Thomas Woodrow, a Presbyterian minister. Wilson's mother, Janet "Jessie" Woodrow Wilson (1830–88), had attended the Presbyterian Female Seminary, and his father, Joseph Ruggles Wilson (1822–1903), was also a Presbyterian minister. Wilson was most influenced by his father, who stressed religious devotion and the power of words.

The young Wilson's health often interfered with his education: On account of illness, he was forced to drop out of Davidson College after only a year. After a twelve-month recovery, he entered the College of New Jersey (now Princeton University) in 1875, and graduated thirty-eighth out of 167 students. In 1879, he entered the University of Virginia Law School. Again, his poor health forced him to withdraw in the second year. He completed his work at home and was admitted to the bar in October 1882. Wilson distinguished himself at Johns Hopkins University as a graduate student in political science. There, he wrote *Congressional Government*, a book that analyzed the constitutional system of checks and balances, and found the system lacking. The book won Wilson scholarly acclaim.

On June 24, 1885, Wilson married Ellen Louise Axson (1860–1914) in a ceremony performed jointly by his father and her grandfather, the Reverend I.S.K. Axson.

This portrait of Woodrow Wilson (above) was painted in 1879, during Wilson's senior year at Princeton. Wilson was a devoted student. He acquired his love of literature from his father, who spent his evenings reading aloud to the family from the works of Charles Dickens and Sir Walter Scott.

Woodrow Wilson's boyhood fascination with trains is pictured here (opposite, top) in a childhood sketch.

This picture (right) shows young Wilson (holding his hat) with friends from Princeton who were members of the "Alligator Club," a fraternal organization common to Ivy League colleges.

SCHOLAR AND GOVERNOR

From 1885 to 1888, Wilson taught political economy and public law at the newly opened Bryn Mawr College. At Wesleyan University in Middletown, Connecticut (1888–90), he taught history and coached the football team. During this time he also commuted weekly to give lectures at Johns Hopkins University. He finally settled at Princeton, where his oratory skills quickly made him the most popular professor on campus. In 1902, he was unanimously appointed president of the university.

The professional politicians who controlled the Democratic Party in New Jersey wanted a candidate who was both personally popular and naive about politics. These "bosses" nominated Wilson for governor, thinking he would be easy to control. After being elected governor of New Jersey in 1910, Wilson proved the bosses wrong. He showed his independence by securing the passage of reform legislation.

Encouraged by his success as governor, Wilson campaigned for president. After several convention ballots, Wilson received the support of influential party leader William Jennings Bryan. This support clinched the Democratic nomination for Wilson.

Wilson was not especially popular with the American public—he seemed a little elite. But a split in the Republican vote, between William Howard Taft and Theodore Roosevelt, enabled Wilson to win the 1912 election.

This picture of Woodrow and Ellen Louise Axson Wilson (above) was taken while Wilson was president of Princeton University. Ellen Wilson was her husband's business partner throughout his career. She proofread and made suggestions for his articles and books and, later, for his political speeches.

Soon after being elected governor of New Jersey, Wilson began stumping the country as a presidential candidate. These pictures (right) show Wilson enthusiastically addressing crowds in Bradford, Ohio; Marion, Indiana; and Sioux City, Iowa.

Addressing a crowd at Bradford, Ohio

A remarkable gesture of restrained enthusiasm

A characteristic expression of resolution

Welcoming the citizens of Marion, Indiana

Greeting a Sioux City delegation from an automobile

A serious speech to students of Morningside University at Sioux City, Iowa

GOVERNOR WILSON IN THE WEST

Snapshots of the Democratic candidate for the Presidency made during his recent tour

WILSON
TAKES OFFICE

Wilson had an enormously successful first year in office, passing legislation that would greatly expand the powers of the executive branch. He stuck to his campaign promise and lowered the import tax, passing the Underwood Tariff Act in 1913. He also supported the Sixteenth Amendment to the Constitution, which provided for a national income tax. Wilson helped engineer the Federal Reserve Act, which created the governing board that oversees interest rates and other banking procedures to this day. In 1914, Wilson pushed for the Clayton Antitrust Act, the first piece of federal legislation to recognize labor unions as rightful organizations.

On August 6, 1914, only eighteen months after Wilson's inauguration, his wife, Ellen, died of Bright's Disease. Soon after Ellen's death, Wilson met Edith Galt (1872–1961). They were married nine months later. There was much gossip about the president's disrespect for the memory of his first wife, and even rumors that he and Mrs. Galt had murdered the First Lady.

The Mexican Revolution was the first of Wilson's international woes. On March 9, 1916, Mexican revolutionary Francisco "Pancho" Villa invaded the town of Columbus, New Mexico, killing eighteen Americans. Wilson sent General John J. Pershing into Mexico to round up Villa and his men. Pershing failed to find them, and Villa's presence only created more tension between the United States and Mexico.

In 1916, Wilson urged Congress to pass reform legislation. This picture shows President Wilson signing the Child Labor Law, which made it illegal to ship products of child labor across state lines. When this law was declared unconstitutional by the Supreme Court, Congress quickly passed another law, which used taxes to discourage child labor.

WOODROW ON TOAST.

President Woodrow Wilson, U.S.A. "IF YOU DON'T TAKE CARE, I SHALL HAVE TO TREAT YOU THE SAME WAY AS EUROPE TREATS THE TURK."

Mexico. "AND HOW'S THAT?"

President Woodrow Wilson. "WELL, I SHALL HAVE TO—TO GO ON WAGGING MY FINGER AT YOU."

This cartoon, published in Punch, mocks the uselessness of the warnings that President Wilson gave Mexico against aggression in U.S. territory.

In the spring of 1914, Ellen Wilson (left) took a bad fall in her bedroom from which she never fully recovered. By the summer, she was confined to her bed after being diagnosed with Bright's Disease, a fatal kidney disorder. When she died, Wilson cried out, "Oh my God, what am I going to do?"

Seven months after his wife's death, Woodrow Wilson was introduced to Edith Bolling Galt (below, right) by his cousin, Helen Woodrow Bones. Immediately after their first meeting, Wilson began courting Miss Galt. He wrote her many love letters and even had a private phone line set up between the White House and her home so that they could speak privately whenever they wanted.

This newspaper illustration (below, left) celebrated Wilson's marriage to Edith Bolling Galt. Not everyone was happy about this match. Some of Wilson's political advisers feared that the president's marrying so soon after his first wife's death would damage his reputation and hurt his chances for reelection in 1916.

WILSON: WORLD WAR I

The most serious issue in Wilson's first term was the outbreak of war in Europe in 1914. Wilson appealed to the American people to remain neutral. The Democratic Party slogan "He kept us out of war!" helped win Wilson the reelection in 1916.

Wilson maintained the call for neutrality into his second term. On May 17, 1915, a German submarine torpedoed and sank a British liner, the *Lusitania*, killing 1,200 passengers including more than 120 Americans. American protest of this attack prompted Germany to call a temporary halt to all submarine warfare. However, by 1917, Germany resumed the practice. Wilson went before a joint session of Congress to ask for a declaration of war against Germany. On April 6, 1917, the Congress voted overwhelmingly to declare war. Asserting that "the world must be made safe for Democracy," Wilson led the United States in the war effort.

Well before the end of the war, Wilson began to plan for peace. In a speech to Congress on January 8, 1918, he outlined the Fourteen Points, his summary of international conditions for keeping order throughout the world. Central to these arguments was the idea of a League of Nations. The League of Nations was to be an organization of countries designed to protect the territory and political independence of its member nations.

"PUTTING ONE OVER"

This 1916 cartoon (above) shows President Wilson swinging the bat of "demand" and missing the ball of "evasion" that was pitched by Kaiser Wilhelm of Germany. The cartoon refers to Wilson's efforts to keep the United States out of World War I.

For Woodrow Wilson (opposite, top), the League of Nations was more than a concept: He felt it was God's will. Shortly before his death, he spoke passionately about the issue, "I have seen fools resist Providence [fate] before, and I have seen their destruction . . . That we shall prevail is as sure as God reigns."

This photograph (right) by H. E. French shows President and Mrs. Wilson enjoying the opening day of the baseball season in 1916.

Opening game 1916 Bx 11?

THE LEAGUE OF NATIONS

The armistice, or peace treaty, which ended World War I, was signed on November 11, 1918. Wilson sailed to Europe to represent the United States in person at the Paris peace conference. This trip was a startling break with tradition: No American president had ever before traveled to Europe.

The conference produced the Treaty of Versailles on June 28, 1919. The treaty was mainly concerned with how Germany would repay the countries it had attacked and ravaged. It also provided, however, for the establishment of the League of Nations.

Wilson began to lose popularity during his absence. The Democratic minority in the Senate still supported Wilson; however, Republican senators were split into two groups. The first group of Republicans, led by Massachusetts senator Henry Cabot Lodge, wanted to ratify the treaty and discuss the League of Nations as a separate issue. The second group, called the "irreconcilables," refused to even consider the League.

When the Senate refused to ratify the treaty as a package, Wilson took his appeal directly to the American people. He embarked on a whirlwind speaking tour that took him to thirty cities in twenty-four days.

In the spring of 1919, Wilson (above) traveled to Paris to join Georges Clemenceau (1841–1929) of France, Vittorio Orlando (1860–1952) of Italy, and David Lloyd George (1863–1945) of England in writing the Treaty of Versailles. Wilson clashed with Clemenceau, who grumbled, "President Wilson and his Fourteen Points bore me. Even God Almighty has only ten."

This 1919 cartoon (right) titled "A Sermon at Rheims" shows Woodrow Wilson and Uncle Sam paying homage to the casualties of the war in a devastated French cathedral. The cathedral's destruction symbolizes the damage that Germany did to France during World War I.

51

WILSON'S HEALTH DECLINES

After making a speech in Pueblo, Colorado, Wilson suffered a mild stroke and was forced to abandon the tour. He returned to Washington and suffered a second, more severe stroke, which left him paralyzed on his left side.

Over the next months, the president was bedridden and would only receive messages through his wife. Edith Wilson carefully studied all matters of state and decided which issues should be brought to his attention. She would then present the problem to the president and communicate his answers to the cabinet and Congress. This mysterious interaction caused Congress and the American public to speculate about who was really making the decisions. For this reason, Edith Wilson has been referred to as the nation's first "lady president."

In 1920, the Senate refused to ratify the Treaty of Versailles. Wilson's increasing unpopularity spelled the end for the power of the Democratic Party. Republican Warren G. Harding defeated Democrat James M. Cox for president (both Harding and Cox were senators from Ohio). An ailing Wilson retired to his home in Washington, D.C., where he died on February 3, 1924. He was buried at Washington Cathedral, the only president buried within the District of Columbia.

This photograph (above) shows Woodrow Wilson sharing a tender moment with his granddaughter Ellen Wilson McAdoo. Ellen was the daughter of Wilson's youngest daughter, Eleanor Randolph Wilson, who married William G. McAdoo (1863–1941).

Chief Lemeuel Occum Fielding, Mrs. Myrtice Germaine, his daughter, and Everett Fielding, his son (opposite, top), visited an ailing President Wilson in 1920. Fielding insisted on visiting the White House in traditional dress. A savvy negotiator, he made a pitch for the preservation of tribal lands in Norwich, Connecticut, while prescribing "bonest" tea to the ailing president, to be taken cold in the morning and hot at night for three days.

This memorial (right) pays tribute to Woodrow Wilson. In The Ordeal of Wilson, *published in 1958, Herbert Hoover wrote, "Three qualities of greatness stood out in Woodrow Wilson. He was a man of staunch [strict] morals. He was more than an idealist; he was the personification of the heritage of idealism of the American people. He brought spiritual concepts to the peace table. He was a born crusader."*

WARREN HARDING

Warren Gamaliel Harding was born on November 2, 1865, at the family farmhouse in Blooming Grove, Ohio. He was the first American president to be born after the Civil War. Both his parents, Phoebe Elizabeth Dickerson Harding (1843–1910) and George Tryon Harding (1843–1928), were doctors.

Harding entered Ohio Central College in Iberia, Ohio, at the age of fifteen. He graduated with a B.S. degree in 1882. Harding married Florence Mabel Kling DeWolfe (1860–1924) on July 8, 1891.

In 1884, Harding and two friends purchased *The Marion Star*, a local newspaper, for $300. Mrs. Harding became the *Star*'s circulation manager and took over the business side of the paper. Her efficiency and management skills made the paper a financial success.

Harding quickly became popular in Ohio Republican circles. He served as state senator from 1899 to 1903. In 1903, Harding was elected lieutenant governor under Governor Myron T. Herrick (1854–1929). He made an unsuccessful bid for governor in 1910. In 1914, Harding defeated the incumbent Ohio senator Joseph Foraker (1846–1917), finally winning the Republican nomination for governor. He defeated Democratic state attorney general Timothy Hogan in the general election.

This photograph (above) taken in 1882 shows a sixteen-year-old Harding. After graduating from college in 1882, Harding spent one term teaching school before he resigned, saying, "It was the hardest job I ever had."

Warren Gamaliel Harding was born in this farmhouse (opposite, top), in Corsica, Ohio. He was the seventh president to emerge from Ohio, all of whom were members of the Republican Party.

The Marion Star *(right), a local Ohio newspaper, was Warren Harding's first commercial venture as a young man.*

HARDING
TAKES OFFICE

Warren G. Harding arrived at the Republican Convention of 1920 as a long shot for the presidential nomination. General Leonard Wood, Governor Frank Lowden of Illinois, and Senator Hiram Gardner of California all had more votes than Harding, but none had a majority. Party leaders held an all-night meeting attempting to reach a compromise. In the end, party leaders chose Harding because, unlike the others in the field, he had no strikes against him. He was popular, he had no political enemies, and he was from a state (Ohio) that was important for the Republicans to win. Harding and Massachusetts Governor Calvin Coolidge (1872–1933) easily defeated James M. Cox and his running mate, Franklin D. Roosevelt (1882–1945).

Harding's policies stressed a return to a simpler, nineteenth-century America dominated by small-town values—something Harding called "normalcy." Harding accidentally coined "normalcy" when he mispronounced "normality" during a campaign speech.

On June 20, 1923, Harding set out on a cross-country tour to meet the American people in person. He particularly enjoyed his visit to Alaska; he was the first president to visit there. On his return trip to Washington, he suffered a heart attack. His condition grew worse. While recuperating at the Palace Hotel in San Francisco, Harding suffered a massive stroke and died on August 2, 1923.

The advances in American technology posed new challenges to the president. This photograph (above) shows Harding (right, seated) meeting with Henry Ford (far left) and Thomas Edison (near left) to discuss the safety of automobiles.

Warren Harding once said, "I like to go out into the country and bloviate." By "bloviate" Harding meant that he liked to make speeches and talk with the American public In 1923, he took a cross-country trip in order to meet the voters. The trip extended as far north as Alaska (opposite, top).

In this photograph (right), Mrs. Harding greets the wives of the Philippine delegation at the White House. The delegation had traveled to Washington, D.C., to secure recognition of the complete independence of the islands. Not until 1934, however, did Congress pass the Tydings-Mcduffie Act, which promised Philippine independence in 1946.

THE HARDING SCANDALS

After Harding's death, a number of scandals became public and discredited the administration. Secretary of the Interior Albert B. Fall (1861–1944) was found guilty of accepting about $400,000 in gifts and "loans" in exchange for oil rights—to the Teapot Dome land reserve in Wyoming and to the Elk Hills land reserve in California. The director of the Veterans Bureau, Charles Forbes (1880–1954) was found guilty of skimming profits from the Bureau, receiving kickbacks from purchases of government supplies, and diverting alcohol and drugs from veterans hospitals to bootleggers and narcotics dealers. Attorney General Harry M. Daugherty (1860–1941) had inside knowledge of these scandals, as well as of wrongdoing in the Justice Department.

Harding's own reputation was tarnished when it was discovered that he had had an extramarital affair with Nan Briton. Nan had given birth to Harding's daughter, Elizabeth Ann Christian, in October 1919. She gave a detailed account of the affair in an exposé she wrote in 1927 titled *The President's Daughter*. In 1963, another Harding affair came to light when dozens of love letters that Harding had written to Carrie Fulton Phillips, wife of his friend James Phillips, were discovered.

This photograph (right) shows (from left to right) former Secretary of the Interior Albert B. Fall (1861–1944) with Edward Doheny (1856–1935), an oil baron, and attorneys Frank J. Hogan and Mark B. Thompson. Fall was found guilty of accepting $400,000 in gifts and "loans" to lease naval oil reserves to Doheny and Henry F. Sinclair (1876–1956), another noted oil producer.

This cartoon (below) by C. K. Berryman, titled "Juggernaut," shows President Harding being chased by the huge scandal of Teapot Dome.

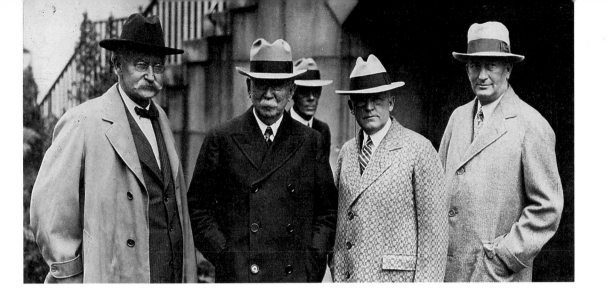

CALVIN COOLIDGE: THE EARLY YEARS

John Calvin Coolidge was born at home on July 4, 1872. The house was located next to the family's general store in Plymouth, Vermont. His father, John Calvin Coolidge, was truly a jack-of-all-trades: farmer, store owner, public official, notary public, and justice of the peace. The senior Mr. Coolidge administered the oath of office to his son, the only father of a president to perform such a role. His mother, Victoria Josephine Moor Coolidge (1846–85), died when Calvin was only twelve. Six years later, his father married Carrie A. Brown.

Coolidge spent his boyhood in Vermont. He attended Amherst College and graduated *cum laude* in 1895. Although Coolidge did not formally attend law school, he studied law privately, at the office of John C. Hammond and Henry P. Field in Northampton, Massachusetts, and was admitted to the bar in 1897.

On October 4, 1905, Coolidge married Grace Anna Goodhue (1879–1957). Grace Coolidge, who taught deaf children, had a relaxed, informal manner that complemented Calvin Coolidge's reserve. The couple settled in Northampton, where Calvin steadily rose through the Republican ranks in local politics. Beginning with a stint on the Northampton city council in 1899, Coolidge worked his way up to become governor of Massachusetts by 1919.

This photograph (right) shows Calvin and Grace Goodhue Coolidge and their two sons, Calvin Jr. and John, at their home in Northampton, Massachusetts. While Coolidge was a member of the Massachusetts legislature and later governor of the state, he rented a room at the Adams House in Boston during the week and returned home to see his wife and children on the weekend.

It was in the house adjoining this store (below) in Plymouth, Vermont, that Coolidge was born. The family also owned a small farm, where Coolidge performed such tasks as splitting firewood, planting corn, and collecting sap from maple trees. His father, John Calvin Coolidge, said, "It always seemed as though Cal could get more sap out of a maple tree than any other young boy I knew."

"SILENT CAL"

During Coolidge's term as governor, the Boston police department formed a union and joined the A.F.L. (American Federation of Labor). The police commissioner refused to recognize the union, and the force went on strike. At first, Coolidge was hesitant to intervene, but when tension increased, he took a firm stand against organized labor. No striker was allowed to return to the force.

Coolidge's hard line with the Boston police brought him national attention and the vice-presidential nomination. After Harding's death on August 2, 1923, Coolidge became president. He was then elected in his own right in 1924.

Although he was a man of few words, "Silent Cal" was quoted often. Stories describing his quiet manner quickly spread. One of the most popular anecdotes was about a socialite who bet a friend that she could entice the president to say more than three words. After failing to draw him into conversation several times, she told him about the wager, and he replied, "You lose."

Coolidge favored minimal government involvement in the economy. Stating that "the chief business of America is business," Coolidge allowed American industry to have free rein. The financial boom of the 1920s—the result of unregulated business and stock speculation—was referred to as "Coolidge Prosperity."

A stoic, resolved Calvin Coolidge faces the nation in this official presidential portrait (above).

The determined handling by Calvin Coolidge of Boston's 1919 police strike is commended in this political cartoon (opposite, top). Coolidge is portrayed alone, manning the ship of Law and Order against a crushing tide of police Anarchy.

This memento (right) shows the Republican party's winning team of Harding and Coolidge on their inauguration day in 1921.

Part II
The Great Depression and World War II

This unfinished portrait of Franklin Delano Roosevelt was commissioned in April 1945, while the president was getting some much needed rest in Warm Springs, Georgia. Roosevelt suffered a massive stroke and died on April 12, 1945, before the painting could be completed.

The stock market crash of 1929 led to a national economic crisis known as the Great Depression. Millions of people lost their jobs and then their homes, unable to meet their mortgage payments or pay the rent. Banks failed and thousands of businesses closed. Although he passed more legislation than any previous president during a depression, Herbert Hoover was unable to rally the ailing U.S. economy. The Depression made the once popular Hoover a villain to the American people. As one discouraged citizen remarked, "If you put a rose in Hoover's hand, it would wilt." Hoover was easily defeated by Democratic challenger Franklin D. Roosevelt.

During his unprecedented twelve-year presidency, Franklin Roosevelt greatly expanded the powers of the executive branch. He distinguished himself through the achievements of the New Deal—a set of policies that invested billions of government dollars in roads and public works, putting tens of thousands of unemployed Americans to work in the process.

As commander in chief of the armed forces, Roosevelt directed a war on three fronts—in Europe, Asia, and Africa—working closely with Soviet premier Joseph Stalin (1879–1953) and British prime minister Winston Churchill (1874–1965) to design the allied war strategy and, later, the terms for peace. Roosevelt died on April 12, 1945, before he could see the realization of the peace he had worked so hard to achieve.

HERBERT HOOVER: THE EARLY YEARS

THE HIGHEST
SALARIED MAN
OF HIS AGE IN
THE WORLD

Herbert Clark Hoover was born in West Branch, Iowa, on August 11, 1874. His parents, Jesse Clark Hoover (1848–80) and Huldah Minthorn Hoover (1848–83), were poor Quaker farmers. Due to the early deaths of his parents, young Hoover became an orphan at age nine. He was passed from relative to relative before traveling by wagon train to Oregon to live with his uncle, Dr. John Minthorn.

Hoover graduated from Stanford University in 1895, with a degree in mining engineering. He married Lou Henry (1874–1944) on February 10, 1899. He then embarked on a twenty-year career as a mining engineer, in which he traveled all over the world and acquired a large fortune.

After the outbreak of World War I in Europe, American officials in London asked Hoover to head the American Relief Commission, which was responsible for helping 120,000 Americans stranded in Europe to return home. Later, as head of the Commission for the Relief of Belgium, Hoover organized the feeding of 10 million people in German-occupied Belgium and France. After America's entry into the war, he served as U.S. food administrator, a post which gave him broad powers over the price, production, and distribution of food. Hoover urged the nation to conserve, and the term "Hooverize" came to mean saving and doing without.

This 1897 news article (above) acclaims a twenty-two-year-old Herbert Hoover as "the highest salaried man of his age in the world." Recently graduated from Stanford University, Hoover received a salary of $83,000 a year as a mining engineer exploring China on behalf of British firms.

This painting (opposite, top) by Grant Wood renders Herbert Hoover's birthplace in West Branch, Iowa (the house is foreground, center) in the deco style popular in the twenties. Hoover felt the painting made his birthplace seem too fancy. Hoover insisted, "We ground our own wheat at the mill; we slaughtered our own hogs for meat; we wove at least part of our own clothing; we made our own soap."

Herbert Hoover (right, in long coat) gained international recognition for his humanitarian work during World War I. He began by heading the American Relief Commission in 1914, which aided Americans stranded in Europe. Later, Hoover organized aid to other countries through the Commission for the Relief of Belgium (1914–19) and the American Relief Administration (1919–20).

HERBERT HOOVER: THE PRESIDENCY

Hoover's political career began in 1921 when he was appointed secretary of commerce by President Warren Harding. In 1928, as the Republican nominee, Hoover easily defeated the Democratic candidate, New York governor Al Smith (1873–1944).

Like most Americans, Hoover was unprepared for the stock market crash of October 29, 1929. By the end of 1929, the crash had caused financial losses estimated at $40 billion. Hundreds of factories had shut down. By 1932, thirteen million Americans were out of work; many were unable to feed or clothe their families, or even keep a roof over their heads.

Hoover expected businesses to solve their own economic problems. However, in 1932, Hoover instructed Congress to take action through programs such as the Reconstruction Finance Corporation, mortgage assistance to farmers and homeowners, public works programs, and the Agricultural Marketing Act.

But the Depression proved to be too much for Herbert Hoover. At the end of his term of office, banks began to fail as a nationwide panic set in. The devastating economic depression that followed made Hoover a traitor in the eyes of many Americans. Ramshackle houses set up by homeless Americans were dubbed "Hoovervilles" by the press. In his 1932 reelection bid, he was soundly defeated by the Democratic opponent, Franklin D. Roosevelt.

In his acceptance speech at the Republican Convention, Hoover looked forward to a prosperous future, saying, "We in America today are nearer to the final triumph over poverty than ever before . . . . The poorhouse is vanishing from among us." This Republican party circular (above) promised "a chicken for every pot and a car in every backyard."

This nonpartisan cartoon (opposite, top) portrays Al Smith and Herbert Hoover as two schoolboys being quizzed on politics and government by a stern Uncle Sam.

Lou Henry Hoover, the president's wife, inspects two Girl Scouts' cooking skills (right). Mrs. Hoover devoted much of her time to new women's organizations, including the League of Women Voters. In a speech at a 1926 Girl Scout conference, she declared, "I believe that even after marriage it is possible for a woman to have a career."

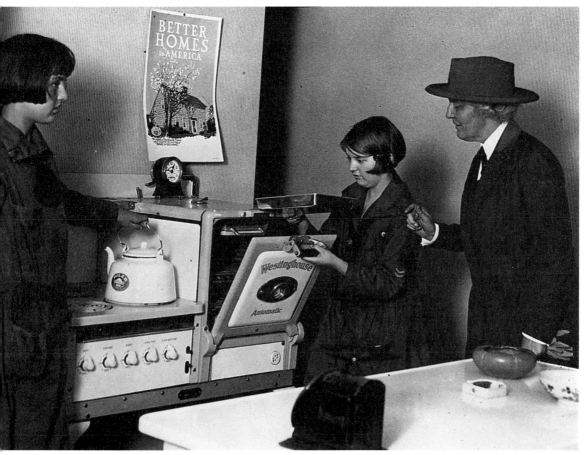

This Hoover family portrait (above) shows Herbert Clark Hoover and Lou Henry Hoover with their sons—Herbert Hoover, Jr. (far left), and Allan Hoover (far right)—and Herbert Jr.'s wife, Margaret Watson Hoover.

On Thursday, October 24, 1929, stock prices dropped dramatically. On "Black Tuesday"—October 29, 1929—the market crashed and billions of dollars were lost. This aerial photograph (right) shows disbelieving stockbrokers pouring on to Wall Street in front of the New York Stock Exchange following word of the crash.

This cartoon (right) mocks Hoover's efforts to end the Depression. Hoover's farm relief programs are depicted as a straw scarecrow designed to scare off hard times.

This 1932 photograph (below) shows young residents of a bonus camp in Washington, D.C. These outdoor camps were common sights during the Great Depression when "Hoover-villes," makeshift dwellings made of packing crates and tarpaper, sprang up across the country. Newspapers were dubbed "Hoover blankets."

HOOVER: THE LATER YEARS

Hoover left the White House in defeat and retired to Palo Alto, California. During his retirement, he remained influential and active in both the Republican Party and the national government. Hoover devoted his spare time to reading, speaking, and writing. He published *The Challenge to Liberty* in 1934, which criticized President Roosevelt's New Deal program. He also wrote his own memoirs, in three volumes, in 1951–52; and *The Ordeal of Woodrow Wilson* in 1958.

After World War II, President Truman appointed Hoover to head the Famine Emergency Committee, a post in which he capably served from 1946 to 1947. His most notable achievement was serving as chairman of the two "Hoover Commissions." In 1947, President Harry S. Truman appointed him chairman of the Commission on the Organization of the Executive Branch—a committee designed to make the presidential sector of government more efficient. Under President Eisenhower, Hoover was appointed to the Commission on Government Operations, which he chaired from 1953 to 1955. The commission proposals that were adopted cut out unnecessary government spending, helping to make the government less costly to the public. Hoover died on October 20, 1964, at the age of ninety.

This 1932 cartoon (above) shows the Republican Party (G.O.P.) prodding Herbert Hoover onto the campaign trail. The Depression made Hoover extremely unpopular with the American people. Toward the end of the campaign, Hoover made ten major speeches defending his administration. Hoover often faced hostile crowds who jeered him.

This picture (right) shows former president Herbert Hoover with children in Poland in 1946. Throughout his life, Hoover continued his humanitarian efforts. As Chairman of the Famine Emergency Committee, Hoover directed relief in Europe after World War II.

FDR: THE EARLY YEARS

Franklin Delano Roosevelt, the fifth cousin of President Theodore Roosevelt, was born on January 30, 1882, at his family's estate in Hyde Park, New York. His parents were Sara "Sallie" Delano Roosevelt (1854–1941) and James Roosevelt (1828–1900). Young Franklin grew up with all the advantages that money could buy. He frequently accompanied his parents abroad on trips to Europe. When he turned sixteen, he was given a twenty-one-foot sailboat as a birthday gift. James Roosevelt was careful, however, to teach his son that with privilege came the responsibility to help others who were not as fortunate.

Roosevelt attended the Groton Preparatory School and later graduated from Harvard University, where he studied political history and government. At Harvard, he also served as editor in chief of the Harvard *Crimson* newspaper. He greatly enjoyed journalism, and decided to remain at Harvard for an extra year to carry on his duties at the *Crimson*. Roosevelt attended Columbia University Law School from 1904 to 1907, but after passing the bar he dropped out and never completed his degree. On March 17, 1905, Roosevelt married Anna Eleanor Roosevelt (1884–1962), a fifth cousin once removed.

As editor and president of The Crimson, *the Harvard newspaper, Roosevelt (seated on the left, above) urged support for the football team and exhorted fans to cheer louder at games.*

This photograph of Eleanor Roosevelt (opposite, top) was taken in 1905 by newlywed Franklin Roosevelt during a honeymoon stop in Venice, Italy.

Roosevelt was born at home, in an upstairs room of this gracious family house (right) in Hyde Park, New York.

FDR:
EARLY CAREER

In 1907, Roosevelt began work at the law firm of Carter, Ledyard, and Milburn in New York City. A Democrat like his father, Roosevelt proved to be a shrewd campaigner. He was able to pull off an upset victory for a state senate seat in a district the Republicans had controlled for more than fifty years.

During his term as state senator (1911–13), Roosevelt distinguished himself as a bold and skillful political fighter. He supported a federal, uniform divorce law, as well as the women's right to vote. A privileged man of wealth and social stature, he was a Democrat who supported the rights of working people and who refused to take orders from the Democratic Party bosses.

After supporting Woodrow Wilson in the election of 1912, Roosevelt was chosen to be his assistant secretary of the navy. In this capacity, Roosevelt was an early advocate of American intervention in World War I. He resigned the commission in 1920 to become the running mate of James M. Cox (1870–1957) on a Democratic ticket which was defeated.

As assistant secretary of the navy, Roosevelt made a name for himself and was selected as Democrat James Cox's running mate. The Cox-Roosevelt ticket (right) was roundly defeated by Republican Warren Harding.

Although remembered primarily as a national leader and international statesman, Franklin Roosevelt was also a family man. He is pictured here with sons James and Elliot, floating model sailboats on a pond at the family compound in Hyde Park. Roosevelt was also a lifelong enthusiast of sailing.

FDR:
THE 1920s

After the election of 1920, Roosevelt returned to New York City to practice law at the law firm of Emmet, Marvin, and Roosevelt.

Tragedy struck Franklin Roosevelt while he was vacationing in Campobello, New Brunswick, in August 1921. After taking a swim in the ice-cold waters of the Bay of Fundy, Roosevelt experienced severe pain in his back and legs. A few days later, he could not stand or even move his legs. His back, arms, and hands were partially paralyzed. The condition was diagnosed as poliomyelitis, commonly called polio. For the rest of his life, Franklin Roosevelt would have to wear ten-pound leg braces and use a wheelchair. But Roosevelt was determined to fight the disease that crippled him. Through regular exercise, Roosevelt regained the use of his hands and strengthened his arms and shoulders.

In 1924, Roosevelt made a remarkable comeback to national politics by making the speech to nominate Governor Alfred E. Smith of New York for president at the Democratic National Convention. In 1928, Roosevelt himself was elected governor of New York State. It was as governor that he delivered his first "fireside chats," informal radio talks that would later become a hallmark of his presidency.

Franklin Roosevelt (right) delivers a spellbinding nominating speech for Al Smith at the Democratic National Convention in 1924. Despite Roosevelt's splendid oration, the Democrats would nominate the more conservative John W. Davis, who would suffer a humiliating defeat at the hands of his Republican opponents.

Journalists take a jab at the political alliance of FDR and Al Smith in this 1932 cartoon (opposite, bottom). The cartoon makes a mean-spirited reference to Roosevelt's disabling polio, with Al Smith sighing in relief that ". . . at least there's nothing wrong with Frank's hearing!"

After contracting polio in 1921, Roosevelt worked long and hard to regain the use of his legs. He would never again walk without the aid of braces and two canes. Privately, he often relied on a wheelchair to move around. His wheelchair (below) was made from a kitchen chair.

ELEANOR ROOSEVELT

Anna Eleanor Roosevelt was born in New York City on October 11, 1884. Her parents were Anna Hall Roosevelt and Elliot Roosevelt, the younger brother of former president Theodore Roosevelt.

Eleanor was a shy child who suffered a lonely upbringing, despite financial privilege. Her mother died of diphtheria when she was eight, and her father, who suffered from alcoholism, died two years later in 1894.

In 1905, she married Franklin Delano Roosevelt in a much publicized ceremony at which then-president Theodore Roosevelt gave the bride away. When Franklin Roosevelt was stricken with polio, Eleanor was by his side in his efforts to recover.

Eleanor Roosevelt used her position as First Lady to advance the causes she believed in. She became active in promoting the rights of organized labor, civil rights for black Americans, and the rights of neglected children. As First Lady, she wrote a daily syndicated newspaper column, "My Day." Remaining active after Franklin's death, she served two terms as a delegate to the United Nations. During her first term, she chaired the U.N. Commission on Human Rights, which drafted the Universal Declaration of Human Rights and supported the creation of Israel. Eleanor Roosevelt died on November 7, 1962. She is buried next to the president at Hyde Park.

Eleanor Roosevelt's newspaper column, "My Day," began as a simple description of her activities as First Lady. In time, the column changed from a report on White House social activity to a political forum in which Mrs. Roosevelt (above) discussed her views on social issues and world events.

In 1942, Eleanor Roosevelt took a trip to London to visit American soldiers stationed there. During the first part of her trip, she stayed with the British royal family. This picture (opposite, top), taken in the Bow Room at Buckingham Palace, shows (left to right) King George, Mrs. Roosevelt, Queen Mary, Princess Margaret Rose, and Princess Elizabeth.

In 1953, after the election of Dwight D. Eisenhower, Eleanor Roosevelt resigned from her position as U.N. delegate. She spent the next few years working for the American Association for the United Nations, giving speeches on behalf of the U.N. Here (right) she addresses fellow Democrats as one of six speakers at a regional conference in Philadelphia, Pennsylvania.

FDR
TAKES OFFICE

In 1932, Franklin Roosevelt won the Democratic presidential nomination. In a campaign dominated by the Great Depression, Roosevelt promised "a New Deal for the American people." Because of Hoover's widespread unpopularity, Roosevelt won easily, receiving 472 electoral votes compared to Hoover's 59. Roosevelt stated frankly in his inaugural address that, in the event that Congress failed to correct the economy, he would ask Congress for "broad executive power to wage a war against the [economic] emergency."

Roosevelt took the oath of office in March 1933, in the midst of a national banking crisis. He took matters boldly into hand, proclaiming in his inaugural address that, "the only thing we have to fear is fear itself." The new president approached the banking crisis by declaring a bank holiday, which allowed federal inspectors to examine the banks' books. They could then determine which banks were safe to reopen. Roosevelt followed up this action with the Banking Acts of 1933 and 1935. These important pieces of legislation made it illegal for banks to speculate in stocks and bonds. It also established the Federal Deposit Insurance Corporation. The FDIC guaranteed all bank deposits by the federal treasury. These measures, over time, went far to restore public confidence in the economy and in government.

This bumper plate (right) advertised Democratic candidates Franklin Roosevelt and John Nance Garner (1868–1967). The repeal of Prohibition, the Eighteenth Amendment to the Constitution, was part of the Democratic Party platform and is symbolized here by the beer mug. In 1933, this aim was accomplished with the ratification of the Twenty-first Amendment.

This 1933 photograph (opposite, bottom) shows Roosevelt making his electrifying inaugural address in which he declared war on the Depression and urged a wartime spirit of unity, asking Congress to grant him sweeping executive powers.

The Resettlement Administration (RA) was created in 1935 to assist disadvantaged farmers. One of the RA's many programs was to build camps for migrant workers. The woman pictured here is a thirty-two-year-old mother of seven who was staying at a camp in Nipoma, California. The photograph (below) was taken by Dorothea Lange, who became famous for her compassionate photography of poor Western farmers.

ROOSEVELT AND GARNER

1933

"THE ONLY THING WE HAVE TO FEAR IS FEAR ITSELF--"

FDR AND THE NEW DEAL

To meet the challenge of the Depression, President Roosevelt greatly expanded the powers of the federal government. The Roosevelt administration created numerous federal agencies to create jobs by rebuilding the country's "infrastructure" (roads, bridges, schools). These agencies provided electricity to remote rural areas, repaired bridges and highways, and acted collectively as a "watchdog" for the nation's economic progress.

Roosevelt's sweeping reforms ran into opposition from those with a more conservative view of government's role in society. The first major controversy over the New Deal concerned the National Recovery Administration (NRA), an agency established to oversee American business codes. In 1935, a lawsuit involving the NRA went to the Supreme Court, and the Court declared the NRA unconstitutional.

In 1937, Roosevelt asked for a major reorganization of the Supreme Court. One amendment proposed that when a Supreme Court justice reached seventy, a younger judge be appointed to sit alongside him on the bench. The president was accused of trying to "pack" the Supreme Court with judges who supported his policies. While Congress debated the legality of a youthful judge monitoring an aging justice, the Supreme Court approved important New Deal legislation. On July 22, 1937, the Senate defeated the proposal by a vote of 70 to 20.

In 1935, Roosevelt established the Works Progress Administration (WPA) to create jobs for skilled workers. The WPA created the Federal Arts Program, which employed artists, writers, actors, and performers. The project, whose slogan was "Paint America," produced many murals like this one (right).

This 1934 cartoon (opposite, bottom) casts Roosevelt as a doctor who is trying a variety of "New Deal remedies" on an ailing Uncle Sam. The NRA is shown as the biggest bottle, and, by implication, the strongest tonic. Congress is portrayed as a nurse who must follow the "doctor's orders."

In 1934, President Roosevelt told Secretary of Labor Frances Perkins, "There is no reason why every child, from the day he is born, shouldn't be a member of the social security system." In August 1935, Congress passed the Social Security Act, which provided for old-age insurance, unemployment insurance, benefits to the disabled, aid to mothers with dependent children, and pensions to the aged. Pictured here (below) is a social security card.

FDR: THE ROAD TO WAR

The New Deal programs were slowly alleviating the Depression. All of the relief programs, however, cost more money than the government was raising in taxes. By 1936, the national debt had risen to $12 billion. Despite the rising debt, the American people gave Roosevelt a landslide victory over Republican Alf Landon.

When Germany's Third Reich invaded Poland on September 1, 1939, war broke out across Europe. Roosevelt publicly supported neutrality for the United States, despite strong personal support for the allied nations of Great Britain and France. On September 3, 1940, Roosevelt announced an agreement with Britain in which the United States gave the British navy fifty destroyers, in exchange for leases on British naval and air bases. On March 21, 1941, Roosevelt again showed his support for the allies when he signed the Lend-Lease Act, which pledged money and arms to help in the fight against Germany.

The war sparked a conflict between American "interventionists," who favored American aid to the allies, and the isolationists, who opposed any U.S. involvement in the conflict.

In 1940, Roosevelt broke a precedent set by George Washington when he chose to run for a third term. Roosevelt, with Henry A. Wallace (1888–1965) as his new running mate, easily defeated Republican Wendell L. Willkie (1892–1944).

These anti-Roosevelt buttons (above) are from the campaign of 1940. Some people were against Roosevelt's serving a third term because they felt he had been president for too long and was gaining too much control of the American government.

This photograph (opposite, top) shows Roosevelt making one of his famous radio broadcasts. As president, Roosevelt continued to address the nation in informal radio speeches known as "fireside chats."

This cartoon (right) shows Roosevelt and the Democratic donkey racing the Republican elephant. In 1940, Roosevelt, who had sought a "spontaneous draft" from his party's convention, was challenged by Republican Wendell L. Willkie.

FDR: WORLD WAR II

On August 12, 1941, President Roosevelt and Prime Minister Winston Churchill of Great Britain signed the Atlantic Charter, an agreement that looked forward to "the final destruction of Nazi Germany," and promised peace and freedom to all people.

In 1940, Germany, Italy, and Japan had signed a mutual aid pact. Beginning in 1941, the United States government began to reduce trade with Japan, issuing strong warnings against Japanese aggression.

On Sunday, December 7, 1941, the Japanese launched a devastating attack on Pearl Harbor, Hawaii. Over two thousand Americans were killed, 1,200 were injured, and much of the Pacific naval fleet was severely damaged. Stating that this was a day that would "live in infamy," Roosevelt asked Congress to declare war on Japan. Congress declared war on December 8, with only one dissenting vote. On December 11, 1941, Germany and Italy declared war on the United States. In response, the United States declared war on these countries as well.

Roosevelt joined forces with Soviet premier Joseph Stalin and British prime minister Winston Churchill in leading the fight against Germany, Japan, and Italy. Roosevelt, Churchill, and Stalin were known as the "Big Three." During the war, they met regularly to discuss war aims and set strategy.

"AIR RAID! AIR RAID! PEARL HARBOR! THIS IS NO DRILL!" These words were broadcast early Sunday morning on December 7, 1941, alerting the sleeping American fleet of a major Japanese air attack (right). Over 2,000 American sailors were killed within two hours. Congress declared war on Japan the following day, signaling America's involvement in World War II.

This document (opposite, bottom) is President Roosevelt's corrected draft of his message to Congress, in which he asked for a declaration of war on Japan.

This 1943 cartoon (below) depicts Roosevelt's shift in focus from domestic problems to the crisis of World War II. After the passage of the Fair Labor Standards Act in 1938, Congress did not pass any other reform legislation for the rest of the decade. With Republicans controlling the House, the New Deal had come to an end.

DRAFT No. 1   December 7, 1941.

PROPOSED MESSAGE TO THE CONGRESS

Yesterday, December 7, 1941, a date which will live in ~~world history~~ *infamy*

the United States of America was ~~simultaneously~~ *suddenly* and deliberately attacked

by naval and air forces of the Empire of Japan~~, without warning~~

The United States was at the moment at peace with that nation and was

still in ~~continuing the~~ conversation with its Government and its Emperor looking

toward the maintenance of peace in the Pacific. Indeed, one hour after

Japanese air squadrons had commenced bombing in ~~Hawaii and the Philippines~~ *Oahu*

the Japanese Ambassador to the United States and his colleague delivered

to the Secretary of State a formal reply to a ~~former~~ *recent American* message, ~~from the~~

~~Secretary.~~ *While* This reply ~~contained a statement~~ *stated it seemed useless to continue the* that diplomatic negotiations

~~must be considered at an end, it~~ contained no threat ~~and no~~ hint *or* *it* *war or* of

armed attack.

It will be recorded that the distance ~~of Hawaii, and especially~~ of

Hawaii from Japan make*s* it obvious that the~~y~~ attack *was* ~~was~~ deliberately

or even weeks
planned many days ago. During the intervening time the Japanese Govern-

ment has deliberately sought to deceive the United States by false

statements and expressions of hope for continued peace.

THE DEATH OF FDR

The strain of running a wartime administration had worn Roosevelt down. In 1944, Roosevelt said that he wanted to retire, but he felt it was his duty to run again. He wanted to avoid a change in leadership during the war. Republican challenger Thomas Dewey (1902–71) launched an aggressive campaign, stressing the president's ill health and criticizing "the tired old men" who were in charge of the government. With the end of the war against Germany in sight, the American people reelected Roosevelt; he carried thirty-six of forty-eight states and received 432 electoral votes, compared to 99 for Dewey.

By the spring of 1945, Germany was near defeat, but Japan was still fighting hard. In February 1945, the "Big Three" met at Yalta, in what was then the Soviet Union, to discuss postwar plans. At this meeting, it became clear that U.S. and Soviet interests in Europe were beginning to conflict. Roosevelt was anxious; he told Churchill, about "the development of the Soviet attitude."

On March 29, 1945, Roosevelt went to Warm Springs, Georgia, for a long overdue rest. He had prepared a speech for broadcast on April 13. On April 12, the president suffered a cerebral hemorrhage and died. Millions of people throughout the world mourned his death.

President Roosevelt confers with Arab leaders, including the King of Saudi Arabia (right), aboard a U.S. warship on Valentine's Day, 1945. In March, the League of Arab Nations would be established, the first such coalition of notoriously warring Arab states.

This simple obituary (below) lists Franklin Roosevelt at the top of a World War II casualty list. After his death, Roosevelt's body was transported by train from Warm Springs, Georgia, to Hyde Park, New York. Mourners gathered along the train route to say good-bye to the president.

Today's Army-Navy Casualty List

Washington, Apr. 13.—Following are the latest casualties in the military services, including next-of-kin.

ARMY-NAVY DEAD

ROOSEVELT, Franklin, D., Commonder-In-Chief, wife, Mrs. Anna Eleanor Roosevelt, the White House.

Navy Dead

DECKER, Carlos Anthony, Fireman 1c. Sister, Mrs. Elizabeth Decker Metz, 16 Concord Pl., Concord, S. I.

Resource Guide

PICTURES IN THIS VOLUME

2–3 Wilson inaugural, P 4–5 presidential seal, WH 6–7 Capitol, AC 8–9 Map, USGS

Timeline: 10–11 B.T. Washington, P, USZ62-56901 Model T, P; campaign, P, USZ62-59419 12–13 Sanger, P, USZ62-33916; Wilson, MSS 14–15 campaign, P, USZ62-95067; poster, P, USZ62-72736; army, P, USZ62-14459 16–17 Einstein, P, USZ62-60242; Hitler, P

Part I: 18–19 Roosevelt, P 20–21 A. Roosevelt, P, USZ62-25802; birthplace, P, USZ62-7756; family, P, LC-BH832-2028 22–23 rancher, P; book cover, P; detectives, P, USZ62-94011 24–25 Rough Riders, P, USZ62-7626 26–27 cartoon, P, USZ62-34060; E. Roosevelt, P, USZ62-25803; campaign, P, LC LOT4406 28–29 doodle, G; cartoon, P; family, P, USZ62-32238 30–31 cartoon, P; safari, P, USZ62-54764 32–33 house, P, USZ62-31118; Roosevelt, P; Yosemite, P 34–35 essay, MSS; birthplace, P 36–37 cartoon, P, USZ62-13360; inaugural, P, USZ62-91030; cow, P, USZ62-11400 38–39 Taft, P; memorial, P 40–41 Wilson, P, USZ62-85850; club, P, USZ62-28653; train drawing, MSS, LCMS-46029-20 42–43 Wilson, P, USZ62-18195; campaign, P, USZ62-66022 44–45 signing, P, USZ62-32620 46–47 Ellen Wilson, P, USZ62-25806; cartoon, P, USZ62-62993; Edith Wilson, P, USZ62-25808; heart, P, USZ62-17634 48–49 cartoon, P, USZ62-58919; Wilson, P, USZ62-35253; baseball, P, USZ62-11304 50–51

Rhiems, P, USZ62-13652; Paris P, USZ62-7483 52–53 grandchild, P, USZ62-14398; wreath, P, USZ62-42090; Occum, P, USZ62-32728 54–55 masthead, MSS; Harding, P, USZ62-64290; birthplace, P, LC B2-5221-5 56–57 Ford/Edison, P, USZ62-95728; Alaska, P; Philippine ladies, P, USZ62-105415 58–59 cartoon, P, USZ62-8705; fall, P 60–61 family, P, USZ62-32237; birthplace, P, USZ62-29996 62–63 poster, P, USZ62-30552; portrait, AC; cartoon, G 64–65 porch, P, USZ62-58102; *Life* cover, P, USZ62-44092

Part II: 66–67 Roosevelt, P 68–69 news clipping, HHL; birthplace, MMA; relief, HHL 70–71 circular, P; Girl Scouts, P, USZ62-20714; cartoon, P, USZ62-48730 72–73 family, P, USZ62-8982; Wall St., P, USZ62-43690; Hooverville, P, USZ62-19646; cartoon, P, USZ62-12397 74–75 relief, P, USZ62-31539; cartoon, P, USZ62-12750 76–77 *Crimson*, FDRL; honeymoon, FDRL; house, FDRL 78–79 sailboats, P, USZ62-13542; campaign, FDRL 80–81 speech, FDRL; wheelchair, FDRL; cartoon, P, USZ62-14166 82–83 E. Roosevelt, FDRL; royal family, P, USZ62-43401; speech, P 84–85 campaign, FDRL; inaugural, P; Depression, P, US734-9058 86–87 SS card, G; cartoon, P, USZ62-17305; mural, P 88–89 buttons, FDRL; broadcast, P, USZ62-2442; cartoon, P 90–91 cartoon, P, USZ62-17308; speech, MSS; Pearl Harbor, P, USZ62-4353 92–93 list, G; meeting, P, USZ62-65203

SUGGESTED READING

BLASSINGAME, WYATT. *The Look-It-Up Book of Presidents.* New York: Random House, 1984

COOK, BLANCHE. *Eleanor Roosevelt.* New York: Penguin, 1992.

DAVIS, KENNETH. *FDR: Into the Storm.* New York: Random House, 1993.

DEGREGORIO, W. A. *The Complete Book of U.S. Presidents.* New York: Dembner Books, 1991.

WHITNEY, D. C. *The American Presidents*, 6th ed. New York: Doubleday, 1986.

Index

Page numbers in *italics* indicate illustrations